D1476754

ISLAMIC MANDALAS

Sterling Publishing Co., Inc.
New York

About the Illustrator

Klaus Holitzka was born in Neuburg-at-the-Danube, Germany, in 1947. In 1969, after training in an advertising agency in Frankfurt, he began working as a free-lance artist. His sense of shapes and painting styles are among his many techniques that characterize his work. In 1978, he founded his own publishing house. Besides creating traditional paintings, he also graphic designs book covers, maps, and prints.

Library of Congress-in-Publication Data Available

10   9   8   7   6   5   4   3   2   1

Published in 2002 by Sterling Publishing Co., Inc.
387 Park Avenue South, New York, N.Y. 10016
Originally published in Germany under the title
*Orientalische Mandalas: 31 Mandalas mit
Spruchweisheiten orientalischer Mystiker* by Schirner
Verlag, Landwehrstr. 7a, Darmstadt, D-64293
© 1999 by Schirner Verlag. English translation © 2002 by
Sterling Publishing Co., Inc.. Translated from the German
to English by Nicole Franke and Daniel Shea.
Distributed in Canada by Sterling Publishing
c/o Canadian Manda Group, One Atlantic Avenue, Suite
105, Toronto, Ontario, M6K 3E7, Canada
Distributed in Great Britain and Europe by Chryslais
Books, 64 Brewery Road, London, N7 9NT, England
Distributed in Australia by Capricorn Link (Australia)
Pty Ltd., P.O. Box 704, Windsor, NSW 2756, Australia

Sterling ISBN 1-4027-0036-9

The First Type of Love

Beautiful creates in the one who perceives beauty, desire, and everything that creates desire is beloved.

That which is felt as beautiful can either be the outer shape, which means the beauty of the body, or the inner shape, which means the perfection of the spiritual and the beauty of moral predispositions.

Al-Ghazali

From *The Alchemy of Happiness*

Illustration source:
Koran illustration
Iran, A.D. 1313

The Unity of Love

The unity of love is
beyond any kind of form,
and embraces each and every form.

My heart is open to all forms. . .
My religion is the religion of love.

Idn'Arabi

Illustration source:
water plant motif
Kashan, Iran 13th c.

Sufi Prayer

I wish God to empty me of everything and to completely fulfill me with His presence.

The Four Doors of Knowledge

The first door is that one
recognizes himself;
the second that one recognizes God;
the third that one recognizes this
world;
the fourth that one recognizes the
world beyond.

Al-Ghazali

From *The Alchemy of Happiness*

If you wish to recognize yourself,
know that you have been created
from two parts.

One is the outer cover,
which one calls the body
and which can be seen with the outer
eye.

The other is the Inner,
which one calls the Soul,
the Spirit, the Heart, and which
can only be recognized by the inner
eye.

Al-Ghazali

From *The Alchemy of Happiness*

You live in my soul
ever inside.
I am the shell,
you the core deep within.

Rariduddin 'Attar

From *Ilahinama*

Illustration source:
metal plate
Iran, 12th–13th c.

When two, who love themselves
in God,
meet and smile at each other,
their sins blow away,
like dry leaves falling from trees in
autumn.

Mudschâhid

Illustration source:
Arabic detail from
silver pitcher
Iran, 15th c.

There is nothing
that could be nearer to you
than you, yourself.
When you, however,
do not know yourself,
how can you wish to know others?

Al-Ghazali

From *The Alchemy of Happiness*

Think so excessively of God
  that you even forget yourself
entirely,
until you open to the calling—
where caller and call no longer exist.

Rumi

From *Poems*

When one realizes
that God is beauty,
He becomes
beloved to the person
to whom His beauty and majesty is
revealed.
The messenger of God says,
"God is beautiful
and he loves beauty."

Al-Ghazali

From *The Alchemy of Happiness*

Know that everything
will return to its
origin.
The heart, the essence,
must be roused
and be called into life,
in order to find its way back
to its divine origin.

Abd al-Qãdir al-Jilãnì

From that moment on,
when I heard my first
love story, I began
to be on the lookout for you,
and knew not how blind I was.

Lovers do not
meet one day
somewhere.

They have always
been one in
the other.

Rumi

Whoever attains insight
needs no longer the Message;

whoever has reached perception,
needs no longer the insight.

Husain al-Halladsch

From *Kitab at-Tawasin*

Illustration source:
...le motif from Idirne Mosque
...urkey, 15th c.

The Fourth Nature of Love

That one loves
only for the sake
of God and in God
and does not try
to reach for something
different through Him:
this is the highest stage of love,
the most inscrutable and mysterious.
It is possible;
for the exuberance of love
reveals itself in this regard.
Love stems from
the Beloved
onto everything that
is connected to him.
For everything,
remote may it be,
has a relation to Him.

Al-Ghazali

From *The Alchemy of Happiness*

Illustration source:
Bronze plate
Khurasan, Iran, 12th c.

O ur Beloved is the one
who is our origin and ending;
and what we observe
of our Beloved with our physical
eyes is Beauty, which surrounds us.
And each part of our Beloved
that is not visible to our eyes
is the Inner Beauty through which
our Beloved speaks to us.

Inayat Khan

From *The Sufi Message*

Illustration source:
...le motif from Idirne Mosque
...urkey, 15th c.

M an has no end,
for he has no beginning.

Abdul Latif

From *Sur Asa*

Illustration source:
plate motif
Iraq, 9th c.

Good is Love.
Therefore, Love is sacred.

Inayat Khan

From *The Sufi Message*

Illustration source:
flower and leaf motif
on pottery
Iran, 12th c.

You prefer to be content,
to go forth alone.
Yet with others,
you go farther and faster. . . .

One wall, standing alone,
is useless,
yet should one
put three or four walls together,
they will support a roof and keep
the grain dry and safe.

Rumi

Illustration source:
bronze plate
Khurasan, Iran, 12th c.

In that emptiness,
when still without signs,
the Being and the world lay in
the corner of Non-Being,
and there the existence
was far from duality
and very distant from
the dialogue of
"we" and "you."

Absolute Beauty, which
has not yet been seen,
shone onto itself
with its own light.

'Abdur Rahman Dschami

From *Yusuf and Zulaicha*

You think
that I know what I do;
that I belong to myself for one
or even a half of a breath?

As little as a feather knows
what it writes;
as little as a ball
can guess where it
next flies.

Rumi

Know this:
no man has the right faith
as long as he still does not wish
the same for his brother
as he wishes for himself.
He must treat his brother as he wishes
himself to be treated.

Al-Ghazali

From *The Alchemy of Happiness*

W e have one life
  in this world to lead:
to deal with
worldly things and
to reach the highest stage.
The greater the limitations are,
the greater will be
the highest perfection
by overcoming them.

Bhai Sahib

You are the end
and also the beginning;
the outside,
O Exalted One,
and the inside.

Farisuddin 'Attar

From *Ilahinama*

ustration source:
ate motif
hurasan, Iran, 12th c.

The beauty of a thing
lies in the fact that
the possible perfection,
corresponding to its
Inner nature,
emerges.

Al-Ghazali

From *The Alchemy of Happiness*

lustration source:
late motif
znik, Turkey, 16th c.

In God there is
no duality.
In this presence there exists
no "I" and "we" and "you."
"I" and "you,"
"we" and "he"
become one. . .

For in His Unity
there is no distinction;
the search, the path,
and the searcher
become one.

Rumi

Every time when
a light rises from you,
a light comes down toward you.

Kubrã

Illustration source:
Koran illustration
Iran, A.D. 1313

I am He, whom I love,
and He, whom I love,
is me.

Two are we—
in only one body.
As you see me,
so you see Him.
And as you see Him,
you see us both.

Al-Hallāj

Illustration source:
motif with birds and
geometric whirls
Egypt, 14ᵗʰ c.

Love comes from
primeval Eternity
and goes to Eternity.
In eighty thousand worlds,
there is not one
who drinks a sip from it
and does not go at last to God.

Rabi'a al-Adawiyya

From *Legends*

What Do Colors Tell Us?

Interpreting the colors you use to color your mandalas is an important step in your journey to self-discovery and self-healing. They can help you to find, recognize, and release those hidden and trapped feelings, emotions, and fears, enabling you to express yourself clearly. While we color, we are subconsciously picking specific colors which represent what we are feeling at the moment. Below you will find what some basic colors may reveal about yourself. Only look at this list after you have finished coloring *all* of the mandalas in this book. Do not be alarmed if you have some negative representations. They are not judgments about you, but rather simply demonstrate how a color can affect you.

Yellow Positive: sun, light, brightness, joy, contentment, inspiration, development, liberation, wisdom, intellect, imagination, enthusiasm, free spirit. Negative: fear of enclosure, superficial, envious, overestimation of self.

Orange Positive: optimism, energy, zest for life, ambition, joy, activity, tenderness, open-minded, courage, strength, warmth, youthfulness, health, self-confidence. Negative: hatred, impulsiveness, rage.

Pink Positive: romance, affection, devotion, softness, unselfishness, feminine, restraint, tenderness, pleasurable, elegant, willower. Negative: inhibited, defenseless, sentimental, lack of reality.

Purple Positive: super-ego, meditative, spirituality, mystic, magic, inspiration, unity of contrasts, sensitivity, individualism. Negative: sorrow, melancholy, privation, renunciation, aversion.

Blue Positive: security, balance, calm, peace, quiet, tranquility, relaxation, freedom, limitless, longing, loyalty, idealism, unselfishness, reason. Negative: emptiness, boredom, paralysis, naïveté.

Turquoise Positive: friendship, sociability, communication, innovative, self-confidence, grace, charm, humor. Negative: capricious, self-centered, need for recognition.

Green Positive: life, nature, hope, willpower, constancy, balance, growth, new beginnings, recovery, well-being, integrity, perceptive, tenacity, determination. Negative: ambitious, dishonesty, drive for power.

Black/Gray Positive: revival, renewal, dignity, unconquerable. Negative: death, destruction, mourning, lack of movement, sin, fear, loss, threatening, darkness, loneliness, hopelessness, compulsive, aversion.

White Positive: purity, innocence, perfection, virtue, objectivity, sublimity, redemption, reliability, sincerity, love of truth, business instinct. Negative: coldness, abstractive, perfectionist.